JESUS, HERE'S MY LUNCH

Jesus, Here's My Lunch

Published in the United States of America.

Joan Murray Ministries &
Seeds of Hope Worldwide Missions

26340 FM 1736
Waller, TX 77484

281-398-2501

Asher, a curious young boy,
whistled as he walked along
the dusty road to his destination in town.
Today will be hot, he thought
as he wiped the sweat from his brows.
He quickened his steps, looking for shade
under the trees along the road.

Arriving at the seashore,
Asher looked for a fisherman
to buy his two small fish for lunch.
After buying his fish, he found a place
to roast them and then looked for
some bread to complete his lunch.

"I wonder why the large crowds of people are going up the mountainside," It's almost time for the Passover Festival." Asher thought.

Being very inquisitive, he decided
to investigate what was happening.
He asked a group of men why all
the people had gathered.
One of the men told him they
were following Jesus, the Prophet,
who had healed many sick people.
Asher's curiosity grew, so he pressed
his way to the front of the crowd.

Asher listened and looked intently
at Jesus as he tried to figure out
how He healed the sick.
He didn't know anyone who had
healed the sick before.
None of the teachers who ministered
in the synagogue had ever healed anyone.
Asher joined the people as they waited on Jesus.

Andrew, one of Jesus' disciples, looked
and marveled at the crowd following Jesus.
He spotted a young boy looking
around with great curiosity.
Approaching Asher, Andrew smiled
and extended his hand in greeting.
Asher juggled his lunch into his left hand
so he could shake Andrew's hand.

"Hello! What's your name?" Andrew asked?
My name is Asher." What do you have in your bag?"
asked Andrew. "My lunch," Asher grinned. "What's for lunch?"
Andrew said, enjoying his conversation with the young boy.
Asher answered, "Two small fish and five loaves of bread."
Patting him on the shoulder, Andrew slowly moved
through the crowd towards Jesus, surrounded
by the other disciples.

When Jesus looked over the large crowd
of people, who were hot and hungry,
He turned to Phillip, another one of His disciples.
Jesus asked, "Phillip, where shall we buy
bread for these people to eat?"
He was testing Phillip to see if he had enough
faith to believe for enough food to feed all the people.

Phillip answered Jesus,
"It would take a lot of money to buy
enough bread for each one to have a bite!"
Andrew spoke up. "There is a young boy
here with his lunch. It's five small loaves and
two small fish, but how will that small lunch
feed all these people?"
Andrew, like Phillip, doubted.

Andrew approached Asher with a broad smile.
Hello again, Asher, Andrew said.
"Jesus would like to know if he can have
your lunch to feed the people."
"Really!" Asher exclaimed in surprise as
he immediately handed over his lunch.

As Asher looked around,
he saw the thousands of people who
had gathered, looking tired and worn.

In total wonder and amazement, Asher thought,
"Jesus will use my lunch of only two fish and
five small loaves to feed all these people. Wow!"

Asher, overwhelmed with joy, witnessed
a miracle unfolding before his eyes.

This I must see. Asher rubbed his hands
together with glee.

He watched with excitement to see how Jesus would use his lunch. Completely captivated by Jesus, Asher watched Him intently.

Jesus said,
"Have the people to sit down."
He took Asher's lunch, thanked God for it,
and gave it to them.

While the people were sitting
on the grass eating, their eyes
widened in disbelief and gratitude at
the amount of food before them.
Asher looked in wide-eyed amazement
as each person received bread. It simply
multiplied as each person received it.
"Wow, wow, wow," Asher exclaimed silently.

Glancing quickly around, Asher was so excited by all the food the people received that he forgot to eat his lunch.

Five thousand men were fed.
They were filled with wonder and
disbelief at what they were experiencing.
After all, Asher got to eat his lunch,
but it was even better because Jesus
had held and prayed over it.
They all ate and were full.

Jesus told the disciples,
"Gather the leftover food."
"Let nothing be wasted." Jesus said.

The disciples gathered and filled twelve baskets with the leftover pieces of the five loaves of bread.

All the people watched in amazement at what Jesus had done. Overwhelmed with emotions after they saw the miracle of the twelve baskets filled with leftover bread, they shouted, "Surely, this is the Prophet Jesus who was to come into the world." Their voices filled with awe and wonder.

Jesus knew they would try to make him king by force, so he slipped away to a mountain alone. Jesus wasn't called to be an earthly king, as the people hoped.

Asher watched in amazement as
they gathered the twelve baskets
full of his leftover bread.
"Man," he said, "How did he feed
all those people with so little."
I don't know of any other prophet
who's done that before.
I bet Jesus is more than a prophet,"
Asher thought.

Andrew and Phillip were both astounded
by the amount of food remaining.
They looked at each other and shook
their heads in awe and wonder.
They had doubted what Jesus could
do with such a small amount of food.

WOW! Andrew exclaimed.
WOW, WOW! Phillip shouted.
Turning to Philip, who looked dumbstruck,
Andrew mumbled, "All Jesus did was pray."
"Phillip, look at what His prayer did!" Andrew could
not find the right words to express the awe he felt.
Still, overcome with surprise, Phillip stared at Jesus
in wonder and amazement. Phillip heard Andrew talking.
The people ate until they couldn't eat another bite!
Yet look, Phillip, we have twelve baskets full of leftover
food, Andrew said quietly.

Andrew and Phillip watched
the people as they went down
the mountainside.
Catching a glimpse of Asher
as he looked at Jesus with wonder,
Andrew approached him again.

"Can you believe that?" Asher exclaimed!
Andrew grinned as he gently stroked his
beard while still trying to wrap his mind
around the fantastic miracle.

Andrew handed some of the baskets
of leftover food to Asher.
Asher stared at the baskets and
him in wonder.

"Son," Andrew said. "You gave
Jesus your lunch, and look at what's left.
"You didn't hesitate to give Jesus all you had."
"Now, receive this abundant blessing for your gift."
"You gave it, and it's being returned to
you in abundance."

With a heart full of gratitude,
Asher lowered his head, overcome
by the abundant blessing his small
lunch had produced for him and the
many who had gathered.

"Thank you," Asher said to Andrew,
unable to contain his awe at
what Jesus had done.

As Asher headed home, he reflected on his day.
"No way," could I have known what would
happen to me today, he exclaimed aloud.
"I can't wait to tell my family and friends
what happened!" "They aren't going to
believe it..." he sighed in wonder.
Asher could barely contain his
excitement as he hurried home.

"Mother, Father," Asher shouted
as he rushed into his house.
"Son, why are you making so
much noise," his mother asked?
"You won't guess what happened
to me today," Asher said joyfully.
"What? His parents asked.

Asher sat down and looked at his parents
as a huge grin crossed his face.
"Well... today, I met Jesus..."

About the Author

Joan Murray is totally committed to helping people discover their destinies. She is the founder and CEO of Joan Murray Ministries and Seeds of Hope Worldwide Missions. Joan is dedicated to teaching, training, equipping and helping people who are in various life struggles.

Joan is a minister, bible teacher, author, and missionary. She has traveled extensively throughout the United States and internationally, sharing the gospel and serving the needs of the oppressed. Joan currently resides in Houston, Texas.

If you would like to know more about Joan Murray Ministries or Seeds of Hope Worldwide Missions, please get in touch with us at:

Joan Murray Ministries & Seeds Of Hope Worldwide Missions

26340 FM 1736
Waller, TX 77848
281-398-2504

email: jmmcontactus@gmail.com
website: joanmurrayministries.org
website: www.jemmuniquegifts.com

**Changing Lives Through the Power
and Truth of God's Word.**

Jesus used a young boy's lunch
to feed five thousand followers.

ISBN 978-1-963016-49-9

52899

9 781963 016499